D0498568

A BOOT UP

THE MOURNE
MOUNTAINS

Steven Hanna

First published in Great Britain in 2009
Reprinted 2014

British Library Cataloguing-in-Publication Data
A CIP record for this title is available from the British Library

ISBN 978 1 906887 06 3

PiXZ Books
Halsgrove House, Ryelands Business Park,
Bagley Road, Wellington, Somerset TA21 9PZ
Tel: 01823 653777
Fax: 01823 216796
email: sales@halsgrove.com

An imprint of Halstar Ltd, part of the Halsgrove group of companies
Information on all Halsgrove titles is available at: www.halsgrove.com

Printed and bound in China by Toppan Leefung

Contents

How to use this book

The Mourne Mountains, located in County Down in Northern Ireland are one of the country's finest and most picturesque areas. Popular with both walkers and climbers, the summits of mountains such as Slieve Donard, Slieve Binnian and Slieve Bearnagh provide both challenging walks combined with rewarding views. The highest peak is Slieve Donard which stands at 849 metres high. One of the main features of the Mourne Mountains is the Mourne Wall, stretching approximately 22 miles and crossing 15 summits. The wall was begun in 1904 and built by hand during the months of April and October; it took 18 years to complete. This Wall is a good way of getting your bearings and most if not all of the walks in this book make reference to it at some stage. The Mourne Mountains are also home to the beautiful Ben Crom Reservoir, Silent Valley Reservoir and Lough Shannagh.

This book contains a mixture of walks, 9 from the Mourne Mountains, and 1 from Tollymore Forest, located on the edge of the Mourne Mountain range. I've chosen a selection of walks for differing ages and abilities and have graded them accordingly. If you are unsure of the area, please stick to the trail which will help minimize your risk of getting lost or getting into difficulty. Also, this book should be used in conjunction with a full OS map of the area, along with a compass or other suitable GPS system.

There are many cases each year where walkers are injured, get lost or find themselves in some other kind of difficulty requiring the assistance of the Mountain Rescue Services. A few simple precautions should help avoid any problems:

- If you are unsure about your fitness, start with the walks graded '1 BOOT' and work your way up to '3 BOOTS'.
- Wear suitable footwear – properly fitted walking boots and good socks are recommended for all the walks.
- Take suitable clothing; the weather in the Mourne Mountains can change very quickly, take a

waterproof and extra warm layers to wear.

- Take plenty to eat and drink en route, dehydration and lack of nourishment can lead to fatigue and mistakes being made. There is nowhere to stop for refreshments en route, so please pack your rucksack accordingly.

- An outline map illustrates each walk but it is recommended that a complete OS map and compass is taken.
- Inform someone of your planned route and expected return time.
- Check the weather forecast in advance and only take to the more challenging routes on clear days.
- And finally, keep to the paths and watch where you are putting your feet — most accidents are caused by careless slips and can often happen on your descent from summits!

Afternoon light in the Mournes, looking towards Slieve Beg and Cove Mountain.

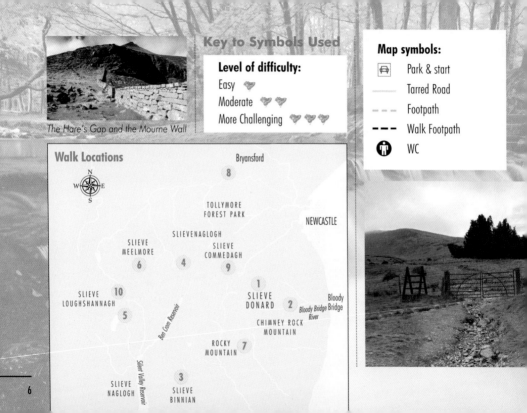

The Hare's Gap and the Mourne Wall

Key to Symbols Used

Level of difficulty:
Easy ❤
Moderate ❤ ❤
More Challenging ❤ ❤ ❤

Map symbols:
🚗 Park & start
    Tarred Road
- - - Footpath
- - - Walk Footpath
🚻 WC

Walk Locations

Bryansford
8

N W E S

TOLLYMORE
FOREST PARK

NEWCASTLE

SLIEVENAGLOGH

SLIEVE
MEELMORE
6

4

SLIEVE
COMMEDAGH
9

1
SLIEVE
DONARD

2 Bloody Bridge
Bloody Bridge
River

Bloody
Bridge

SLIEVE
LOUGHSHANNAGH

10

5

Ben Crom Reservoir

CHIMNEY ROCK
MOUNTAIN

ROCKY
MOUNTAIN

7

Silent Valley Reservoir

SLIEVE
NAGLOGH

3
SLIEVE
BINNIAN

1 Slieve Donard

The highest peak in Northern Ireland, this walk, although challenging, provides you with amazing views over the whole of the Mourne Mountains.

Newcastle
Drinnahilly
1
2
3
4
Thomas's Mountain
Millstone Mountain
Glen Fofanny River
Cliffs
7
SLIEVE DONARD
ne Wall
Bloody Bridge River
Chimney Rock Mountain

This is one of the most popular walks in the Mournes, easily accessible with ample car parking available in Newcastle. Having made the steep climb up to the summit, sit back, have your lunch and enjoy the fine views from Donard's summit.

Level: 🥾🥾🥾
Length: approx 9km
Time: approx 4 – 5 hours
Terrain: Strenuous in places
Nearest Refreshments: Newcastle
Info: Toilets available in car park at starting point

Donard Bridge.

One of the many gorgeous waterfalls in Donard Forest.

① The walk begins in Donard Park (374305) where there is suitable parking beside the football pitches. During the First World War, soldiers were stationed here briefly before being sent to the Somme in France. Donard Park is a very popular starting point for ramblers heading into the Mournes. To begin, you follow the path up the right hand side of the Glen River before entering Donard Wood. The path continues up the right hand side of the river until it reaches Donard Bridge.

② Cross this bridge and then continue up the path, which will now lead you up the left hand side of the river, with many beautiful and breath-taking waterfalls.

The Ice House.

The view from the col between Slieve Donard and Slieve Commedagh, looking back towards Newcastle.

3 Approximately 410 metres further up river you will come to another bridge which you need to re-cross back onto the right hand side of the river and to continue to follow the path up along the side of the river.

4 This path will lead you to another bridge, however, do not cross this one, but remain on the right hand side of the river and follow the path which will eventually lead you to a stile / gateway. By this time, you will have made your way up and out of Donard Wood. As you pass through the gateway, on your left hand side, on the opposite side of the river, you will see the Ice House, an igloo-shaped stone building built by the Annesley family, former owners of Donard Park.

View from the Brandy Pad.

5 Continue along the narrow path as it twists its way up the side of the valley until it eventually reaches a narrow point in the river where you can cross safely. The buttress of Eagle Rock overlooks the river bank. There now begins a steep incline towards the saddle between Slieve Donard and Slieve Commedagh, with Donard being on the left and Commedagh to the right. Amazing views are available looking back down towards Donard Wood with Newcastle and Murlough Bay in the distance. Continue on the path as it winds its way upwards until you reach level ground and eventually the Mourne Wall.

6 At this point, by heading left and following the very steep incline of the Mourne Wall you will reach the summit of Donard at 849 metres high. Behold the highest mountain peak anywhere in Northern Ireland. Slieve Donard is named after a follower of Saint Patrick, known as Saint Domangart (or Domangard). He is the patron saint of Maghera. The view from the summit on a clear day can be outstanding, with the possibility of seeing Belfast 30 miles away to the north.

7 After reaching the summit, your descent is via the same route you followed on your way up. Care should be taken as the descent from the summit of Donard can be quite awkward in places.

Another stunning waterfall in Donard Forest.

2 **Bloody Bridge**

*Everyone must at some time, follow the trail from
Bloody Bridge amongst all the picturesque rock pools
and boulders, high up into the Mournes.*

Level: 🐾 🐾 🐾
Length: approx 10km
Time: approx 5 hours
Terrain: Strenuous in places, with some areas having very loose footing
Nearest Refreshments: Newcastle
Info: Toilets available in car park at starting point

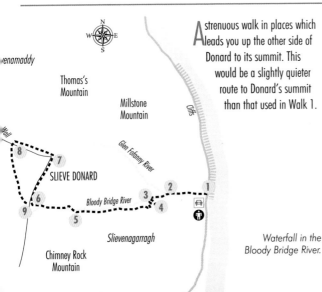

A strenuous walk in places which leads you up the other side of Donard to its summit. This would be a slightly quieter route to Donard's summit than that used in Walk 1.

Thomas's Mountain

Millstone Mountain

Glen Fofanny River

Cliffs

venamaddy

Well

8

7

SLIEVE DONARD

6

9

5

Bloody Bridge River

3

2

1

4

Slievenagarragh

Chimney Rock Mountain

Waterfall in the Bloody Bridge River.

13

Late afternoon light on the Glen Fofanny River.

① The walk begins in the Council Car Park (388270) on the main road between Newcastle and Kilkeel. There are ample parking and toilet facilities available here. After crossing the road, you pass through a gate and stile which has a National Trust sign on it, and begin to follow the National Trust path inland which is on the right hand side of the river. This is a beautiful part of the walk, which takes you past the original Bloody Bridge and the river is full of many waterfalls and deep rock pools, making it an ideal and popular location for wet bouldering. At this bridge, back in 1641, prisoners on their way from Newcastle to Greencastle were massacred.

The Bloody Bridge River, which is a popular spot for outdoor activities such as wet bouldering.

② After approximately 725 – 750 metres, there is a meeting of two rivers, The Bloody Bridge on the left and the Glen Fofanny River on the right. At this point, you should cross over the rocks between the two rivers, and follow the narrow path to the right of the Bloody Bridge River. A short distance after crossing, you will reach a stile, and after this, the path continues to wind and twist its way upstream.

The Mourne Wall, with Slieve Binnian in the distance.

After approximately 410 metres, there is a suitable crossing point where the Bloody Bridge River is very shallow and there are a number of conveniently positioned rocks and boulders that will help you cross over to the opposite bank.

 For a short distance, the path twists back on itself, looking towards the sea. Keep to the path and you will eventually come to a larger quarry track, which heads up through the valley. This section of the path can be quite challenging due to the loose rocks, so adequate care should be taken. An impressive approach up through the valley with Carr's Face and Chimney Rock Mountain on your left, and Leganabruchan and Crossone on your right.

 Continue on up this quarry track, keeping the Bloody Bridge River on your right, and just before you reach the quarry, you veer off right, crossing the river back onto its right bank.

 Continue upwards, now keeping the Bloody Bridge River on your left, and the path will eventually lead you to the Mourne

Panoramic view from the Brandy Pad.

Bloody Bridge and the Bloody Bridge River.

Wall, with the impressive Slieve Donard towering to your right. By following the wall to the right, you will reach the summit of Slieve Donard.

 7 When you reach the summit, follow the other Mourne Wall which takes you down the other side of Donard.

8 When you reach the col between Donard and Commedagh, cross over the wall using the stile, and follow the path left which joins onto the Brandy Pad. By following the Brandy Pad to your left, you will rejoin the Mourne Wall.

 9 Cross the stile and begin your descent to Bloody Bridge using the same route you came up.

3 **Slieve Binnian**

*One of the most popular peaks in the Mournes,
this walk takes you along the impressive summit
of Slieve Binnian*

Level: 🌸 🌸 🌸
Length: approx 11km
Time: approx 5 hours
Terrain: Strenuous in places, with quite a
long yet gradual ascent
Nearest Refreshments: Newcastle

One of the best walks in the Mourne
Mountains, sweeping past the
Blue Lough and then up onto the
large spacious summit of Binnian.
Impressive views of both Ben Crom
Reservoir and the Silent Valley Reservoir
are available from the summit.

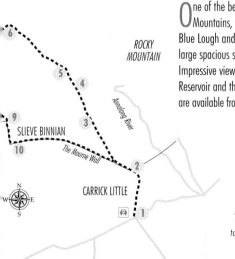

ROCKY
MOUNTAIN

Annalong River

SLIEVE BINNIAN

The Mourne Wall

CARRICK LITTLE

*The view up the valley
towards Slieve Donard.*

① The walk begins at the car park on the Head Road. If coming from Newcastle direction, follow the main coast road between Newcastle and Annalong. Head past the car park at Bloody Bridge, and keep going until you come to a road on the right called the Quarter Road. Turn off here and follow this road which leads onto the Head Road. You will pass Rourke's Park on your right, then go over Dunnywater Bridge, and the Carrick Little car park will then be on your right. In busy months, you may be required to park along the road side as the car park will fill up quite quickly.

② Once arrived, you will begin the walk by following the farm track until you reach a stile and gate approx 1km later. The track is wide and the ascent is quite gradual.

③ After crossing the stile, you will follow the path that leads inland with Annalong Wood on your right. The impressive Slieve Binnian is visible high to your left with Slieve Lamagan towering to its right. Continue on this path, crossing over the Mourne Wall as you begin to leave Annalong Wood behind you. The footing on this section of the path can be quite loose at times so a little caution is advisable.

The Blue Lough.

Views looking down on Ben Crom Reservoir.

4 Continue your ascent until you reach a fork in the path. Keep to the left path as you pass Douglas Crag to your left until you reach a shallow stream which you will need to cross. There is a suitable crossing point yet care should still be taken. To your right are impressive views up the Annalong Valley with the peaks of Slieve Donard and Slieve Commedagh towering far in the distance. To your right you also have views of Hares Castle and Rocky Mountain and to your left you can see Cove Mountain and Slieve Beg.

5 After approx 400m from the last fork in the path, you will reach another fork, and again you follow the left fork, keeping to the left side of the rocky buttress of Percy Bysshe. As you make your way around Percy Bysshe, you will be greeted with a view of the beautiful Blue Lough. At this point, you are sandwiched between Slieve Lamagan (to you right) and Slieve Binnian (on your left).

6 Continue on the path, which will now lead you to the col. High to your left is Buzzard's Roost. Upon reaching the col, you need to take a narrow and winding path to

Panoramic views from Slieve Binnian.

your left, which will eventually lead you up the side of Binnian. This is normally a good spot to enjoy the fine views looking over Ben Crom reservoir and out towards Slieve Bearnagh. This is also an ideal spot to 're-fuel' before the final ascent.

(7) The narrow path winds its way upwards between the heather. Be careful as the path is quite steep in places, and the ground can be very soft and muddy. After a steep beginning, the path does ease off and there is a more gradual ascent up towards the impressive North Tor of Binnian.

Turning around and looking backwards, not only can you still see the Ben Crom reservoir, but Lough Shannagh also comes into view to your left.

(8) Keeping the North Tor on your left, the path sweeps its way round to the right towards the Summit Tor. Down to your left, Binnian Lough is now visible.

(9) The approach to the Summit Tor is quite gradual, passing through an area of the Mourne wall which has been knocked down. At the summit there are impressive views down to the Silent Valley Reservoir and across to Carn Mountain and Slieve Muck.

A break in the Mourne Wall with Slieve Donard visible in the distance.

(10) The descent from the summit is made by following the Mourne Wall (staying to its left hand side) until it rejoins the path at Annalong Wood. Caution should be taken on this descent as it can be quite tricky and awkward in places. It's also an ideal spot to stop and again admire the views up the Annalong Valley towards Slieve Donard and the Brandy Pad. The walk is concluded by following the farm track back to the car park.

The descent from Binnian is steep but the views are amazing.

4 **Hare's Gap**

A relatively easy and short walk with impressive views along the Brandy Pad.

A good starting walk for those new to the Mournes. The short walk gets you into the heart of the mountains, with many great views looking along the Brandy Pad. Once you reach the Hare's Gap, a variety of paths is available taking you further into the mountains.

Level:
Length: approx 7km
Time: approx 2 – 3 hours
Terrain: Easy
Nearest Refreshments: Newcastle

Views of Slieve Meelmore and the rugged tors of Slieve Bearnagh in the distance.

View looking up towards the Hare's Gap.

(1) The walk begins at the car park on the Trassey Road (311314), quite close to the Clonachullion Hill. There is adequate parking; however, in peak times and bank holidays, the car park will fill up quickly so you may have to park along the roadside as this is a very popular starting point for Mourne walkers. In years gone by, goods used to be smuggled from the coast at Bloody Bridge along the Brandy Pad and down by the Hare's Gap. The contraband goods included things such as coffee, spices and soap.

(2) Leaving the car park, turn left and walk a short distance up the Trassey Road until you come to a set of double gates and stile, which indicates the start of the Trassey Track. You will now begin a gradual ascent up a reasonably narrow stoned lane way before you reach a clearing where you will be greeted by a fine view of Slieve Meelmore, Slieve Bearnagh and Slievenaglogh (from right to left). Slieve Meelmore and Slieve Bearnagh are separated by the col at Pollaphuca while the col at the Hare's Gap separates the peaks of Bearnagh and Slievenaglogh.

(3) Again, you will come to a set of double gates and a stile. Please keep the gates closed and use the stile. Continue up the narrow track as it begins a gradual ascent, with better views of the granite cliff face of Spellack, which is part of Slieve Meelmore, to your right. The track provides reasonably good footing, although there may be a few loose stones here and there.

The granite cliff face of Spellack.

The path that leads up along the Trassey River, with Slieve Bearnagh in the distance.

4 You will come to another stile and set of double gates, and then the path begins to wind it's way uphill with the surface becoming a little more loose under foot. The Trassey Track continues to snake its way up towards the Hare's Gap, with the Trassey River running on your right hand side.

5 You will come to a crossing point in the river, which you cross and continue for approximately another 95 metres until you come to a fork in the path.

The view back down the valley towards Slievenaman and Lough Island Reavy Reservoir just about visible in the distance.

6 To veer right would take you up towards the quarry nestled on the side of Slieve Bearnagh. However, you take the left fork, which leads you onto your final ascent up a reasonably steep boulder field to the

Mourne Wall and the Hare's Gap, nestled between Slievenaglogh to your left and Slieve Bearnagh to your right. Care should be taken on this final ascent as the footing can be uneven and slippery. Don't forget to stop and

catch your breath and look back on the stunning views overlooking Slievenaman and Lough Island Reavy Reservoir which will now be visible in the distance. On the final approach, fantastic views are also available of Slieve Bearnagh to your right, which some consider to be the most impressive of the peaks due to its summit tors, crags and smooth rock slabs.

(7) Upon reaching the Mourne Wall, you can then take a variety of different routes. Many choose to follow the Mourne Wall right and climb to the summit of Slieve Bearnagh whilst one of the most popular walks from here is to continue further into the Mournes by following the Brandy Pad.

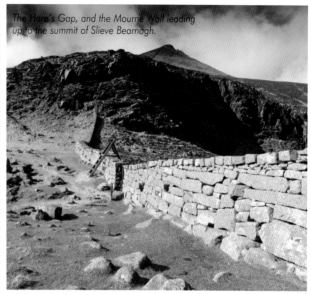

The Hare's Gap, and the Mourne Wall leading up to the summit of Slieve Bearnagh.

A view from the Brandy Pad towards the Hare's Gap and the summit of Slieve Bearnagh.

5 Lough Shannagh

A pleasant walk which provides superb views of the Silent Valley and Ben Crom Reservoirs

Level: 🐾 🐾
Length: approx 12km
Time: approx 5 hours
Terrain: A long walk which requires an adequate amount of fitness
Nearest Refreshments: Newcastle

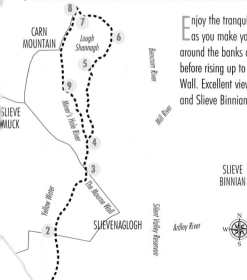

Enjoy the tranquillity of this walk as you make your way along and around the banks of Lough Shannagh before rising up to join the Mourne Wall. Excellent views available of Doan and Slieve Binnian.

CARN MOUNTAIN

Lough Shannagh

Bencrom River

Mill River

SLIEVE MUCK

Miner's Hole River

The Mourne Wall

Yellow Water

SLIEVENAGLOGH

Silent Valley Reservoir

Ardley River

SLIEVE BINNIAN

N
W · E
S

The view up Banns Road after leaving the car park.

① The walk begins at the car park known as the Banns Road car park (284214), which is just off the main Kilkeel to Hilltown Road (B27). Coming from Newcastle. Follow the signs for the Silent Valley. Drive past the entrance gates and you will arrive at a junction at which you will turn right. Continue on the Head Road until you arrive at the junction with the main B27. Turn right and travel a short distance where you will find the car park situated on your right, with Crocknafeola Wood visible to your left. Parking is limited so it's best to get there early.

② The walk begins from the car park by following the Lough Shannagh Track (also known as the Banns Road). A short distance from the car park you will reach a stile and gate. The Yellow Water River will be down to your left and Slievenagore will be on your right. Continue over the stile and stay on the Lough Shannagh Track until you reach another stile and gate at the Mourne Wall. Here, fine views are available looking across to Ben Crom Reservoir. It is nestled between the slopes of Slieve Binnian on its right (look for the huge rugged tors on its summit) and Ben Crom on its left. At this point in the Mourne Wall, if you were to follow it to the left would lead you to the summit of Slieve Muck at 674m. By following it to your right, it would lead you to the top of Slievenaglogh at 445m, which would give you great views of the Silent Valley Reservoir and across onto Slieve Binnian.

Your crossing point on the Mourne Wall.

The view looking towards Doan, Slieve Meelbeg and Slieve Loughshannagh.

3 You need to use the stile to cross the Mourne Wall and continue on the Lough Shannagh Track, crossing over the Miners Hole River. The small bridge you cross is said to date back to 1812.

4 Continue on the track, which veers up and to your right and will eventually lead you to Lough Shannagh. Care should be taken as the path consists of many loose stones and rubble and footing is very uneven. This section of the path leads up through rock and heather, yet offers great views of Carn Mountain, Doan and Ben Crom. As you begin to reach the lough itself, much of the path turns to grit and sand, and can be quite wet in places.

Low cloud rolls in over Lough Shannagh.

The Mourne Wall leading to the summit of Slieve Loughshannagh.

(5) The path reaches a fork, and by taking the left path, will lead you the short distance down to the water's edge.

(6) When you rejoin the path, continue towards the north east corner of the lough where you will find a stone shelter and a dam. Care should be taken in the approach to the dam as the ground can be very wet underfoot. Cross the stream / river just below the dam, and then make your way uphill for a distance of approximately 45m or so until you come to a narrow 'path' which cuts across the slope. The path is very uneven and care should be taken as sometimes the path appears more like a stream than a proper path.

(7) Continue until the path finally reaches a grass slope which will lead you upwards to the Mourne Wall, between Carn Mountain and Slieve Loughshannagh. Again, this section can be very marshy and wet. Upon reaching the Mourne Wall, you have fine views looking over towards Ott Mountain and Butter Mountain.

(8) Turn left and follow the Mourne Wall upwards which will eventually reach the summit of Carn Mountain at a height of 588m. By keeping the wall to your right, continue downwards until you reach a break in the wall where you will veer left at the Miners Hole River.

9 Continue on the left bank of the river which will eventually lead you back to the small bridge you crossed earlier. Follow the Lough Shannagh Track back to the car park, not forgetting to stop and admire the views over towards Slieve Binnian on your left.

The descent from Carn Mountain.

A panoramic view looking back up Banns Road.

6 Slieve Meelmore

A reasonably 'physical' walk in places with superb views looking towards to the rugged tors of Slieve Bearnagh

This walk has quite a steep beginning but well worth it when you reach the summit of Slieve Meelmore. Enjoy the descent down towards Bearnagh before sweeping down onto the Trassey Track.

Level: ♥ ♥ ♥
Distance: approx 8.5km
Time: approx 4 hours
Terrain: Moderate – Strenuous
Nearest Refreshments: Newcastle

Your starting point, looking up towards Slieve Meelbeg.

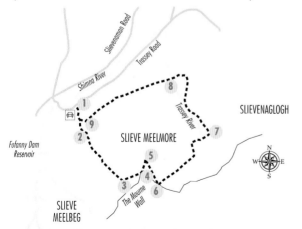

Slievenaman Road

Trassey Road

Shimna River

Trassey River

SLIEVENAGLOGH

1
9
2
8
7
5
4
6
3

Fofanny Dam Reservoir

SLIEVE MEELMORE

The Mourne Wall

SLIEVE MEELBEG

N
W E
S

① The walk begins at the car park on the Trassey Road known as Happy Valley car park (293296). As with most Mourne car parks, space is very limited. The car park itself only holds around 6 or 7 cars, so unless you want to park along the road side, it is advisable to get there early.

Leaving the car park, follow the path that leads to a gate and stile. Cross the stile and continue to follow the stony path uphill. After a short distance, you will notice another stile to your left, on the opposite bank of the stream. This stile actually marks the end point of your walk (to its left you will see a stone wall which runs back around Slieve Meelmore and towards the Trassey River).

② Continue on the path uphill for another 15 or 20 metres, and then descend towards the stream and find a suitable crossing point. You need to cross the stream and follow the wall upwards as it leads you up the valley between Slieve Meelmore (on your left) and Slieve Meelbeg (on your right).

③ This path is very narrow at times, but always keep the stream on your right and keep the wall close on your left. Don't forget to turn around and enjoy the views back to the valley towards the Trassey Road and Slievenaman. As the wall winds its way upwards, the ascent gradually becomes much steeper. The wall takes

Mist comes down through the valley between Slieve Meelmore and Slieve Meelbeg.

The amazing view looking back down the valley towards the Happy Valley car park.

The view up to the summit of Slieve Meelbeg.

a sharp turn to the left as it heads up the side of Slieve Meelmore to meet the Mourne Wall, and it is this section which provides a bit of a physical challenge. But the views will make up for any tiredness or aches and pains in the legs.

When you reach the main Mourne Wall, looking to your right, you can see the wall run right across to the summit of Slieve Meelbeg at a height of 708 metres. You also have great views looking over towards the Silent Valley Reservoir and Slieve Binnian. But one of the best views has to be that of the rugged peak of Slieve Bearnagh straight ahead.

A Belfast Water Commissioner's Tower built in 1921 sits at the summit of Slieve Meelmore.

The view looking down through Pollaphuca towards the Trassey Track.

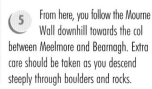

6 When you reach the col, you will find a stile at the wall, which you cross and then descend down a winding path towards the Trassey Track. This area is very popular with rock climbers and is known as Pollaphuca.

7 Upon reaching the Trassey Track, turn left and head downhill, taking extra care as the path is full of loose stones and rocks and your footing is quite uneven. Turning right would take you up towards the Hare's Gap and Brandy Pad. Stay on the path until you reach a stile and gate. There is a stone wall to the left of the stile which stretches out into the distance and is signposted as part of the Ulster Way.

4 You know need to cross the wall and follow it to the left as it rises upwards to the summit of Slieve Meelmore, which stands at a height of 687 metres. At the summit you will see the Belfast Water Commissioner's Tower, dating back to 1921. From here, amazing views of Slieve Bearnagh, Slievenaglogh, Slieve Corragh, Slieve Commedagh and Slieve Donard are possible.

5 From here, you follow the Mourne Wall downhill towards the col between Meelmore and Bearnagh. Extra care should be taken as you descend steeply through boulders and rocks.

The Ulster Way.

8 Don't cross the stile, instead turn left and follow this wall (keeping to its left hand side) and it will eventually bring you back to your starting point.

9 You will reach another stile which you cross, then cross back over the stream and follow the short path back down to the car park.

Your final crossing point before your return to the car park.

7 Rocky Mountain

A less demanding walk than many of the others but one that takes you into the heart of the mountains

This walk provides stunning views up the valley towards Slieve Donard and Slieve Commedagh, and excellent views running parallel to Slieve Binnian. Not the most difficult of walks.

Level: 🥾🥾 🥾
Length: approx 7km
Time: approx 3 hours
Terrain: Moderate
Nearest Refreshments: Newcastle

ROCKY MOUNTAIN

The start of the walk alongside Rourke's Park.

The walk begins where the Quarter Road meets the Head Road (360224) at Rourke's Park. Please park sensibly along the side of the road. At the corner of the road, there is a track leading right which takes you along the edge of Rourke's Park. Follow this track until you come to a gate. Cross through the gate, and then approximately 50 metres later you will come to another gate. Again, pass through, remembering to close the gate behind you.

Immediately after the gate, turn left and follow the line of the wall up the field, and you will see another gate located in the middle of another stone wall in front of you.

Follow the stone wall upwards towards Round Seefin.

The Mourne Wall leading up across Long Seefin towards Rocky Mountain.

Annalong Wood with Slieve Binnian far in the distance to the left.

The intersection of the Mourne Wall.

(3) Again, cross through the gate and immediately turn left and follow the path approximately 10 metres until you meet another wall and stile.

(4) Do not cross the stile. Instead turn right and follow the wall upwards along the track, keeping the wall to your left hand side. The ground is quite firm and this section can be fairly steep in places. As you begin to ascend towards Round Seefin, remember to look back and enjoy the fine views overlooking Annalong and the Irish Sea.

(5) Eventually this winding path will reach a wire fence and stile. Cross the stile and veer right, following the sign and continue on the path which sweeps round and brings

Views of Slieve Donard on the right and Slieve Commedagh on the left.

you back to the wall you were following. To your left, you have amazing views of Slieve Binnian with its North and South Tors.

(6) Follow the wall forward as it stretches out across the relatively flat summit of Long Seefin.

En route you will meet a small tower on the wall which marks the intersection of the Mourne Wall with the wall which takes you back towards Round Seefin. Continue straight ahead, keeping the Mourne Wall to your left and you will eventually come to a stile.

(7) Cross the stile, and from here, you can make the short scramble up to the summit of Rocky Mountain.

(8) (If you were to follow the Mourne Wall from here and not cross the stile, you would eventually reach the summit of Slieve Donard at a height of 853 metres). Alternatively, you can follow the track which snakes its way between Rocky Mountain (to the left) and the Mourne Wall (to the right).

Slieve Binnian on your left.

9. From this track, you have impressive views of the mighty Slieve Donard and Slieve Commedagh.

10. To begin your descent, make your way back towards the Mourne Wall and from the stile, follow the path that leads down and veers to the right. At the start of the path, it is made up of loose boulders and so care should be taken so as not to loose your footing. About half way down, it turns into more of a grassy track, and eventually reaches another stone wall. This path provides stunning views of Slieve Binnian and Slievelamagan.

11. When you reach the wall, turn right and follow it till you reach another wall and stile.

12. Cross the stile and turn immediately left onto the Dunnywater Track. Follow this track, crossing through another gate (remember to use the rope to close the gate behind you) and continuing on until you reach the Head Road. Turn left and a short walk will return you to your car.

8 **Tollymore Forest**

A stunningly beautiful walk along the river in one of Northern Ireland's most picturesque forest parks

For those not ready to venture high up into the mountains, this walk is for you. This peaceful forest is really brought to life as you make your way along the banks of the Shimna River. A great time to visit Tollymore is in the autumn when the colours are changing and the whole place comes to life.

Level:
Distance: approx 5km
Time: approx 2 hours
Level: Moderate
Nearest Refreshments: Forest Café
Info: Toilets available in car park at starting point

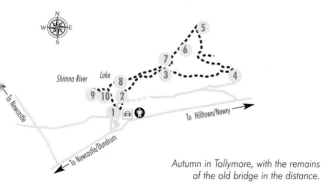

Autumn in Tollymore, with the remains of the old bridge in the distance.

49

(1) Tollymore Forest is nestled at the foot of the Mourne Mountains and has been listed in the top 20 British picnic sites by the *Sunday Times*. With vast camping and caravanning facilities, Tollymore is one of the most beautiful and popular forests in Northern Ireland, covering almost 630 hectares.

(2) The walk starts in the main car park in Tollymore Forest, with breath-taking views looking up into the Mourne Mountains. Follow the red markers leading you down towards the Shimna River. When you reach the river, the River Trail leads you along the right hand side of the Shimna River, passing the remains of an old wooden bridge which was badly damaged during recent flooding and

The Shimna River.

high winds. There are many excellent little nooks and waterfalls to explore and enjoy along this section of the river. Keep following the path and you will arrive at your first set of stepping stones. Continue past these and eventually you will arrive at another set of stepping stones. Just after this is where the Spinkwee River and Shimna River join.

(3) Follow the path as it veers off to the right and you will eventually reach another bridge over the river. Ignore this and keep to the path, with the river still on your left-hand side.

(4) You will pass another set of stepping stones before you come to Parnell's Bridge, which you cross.

5 Immediately after crossing the bridge, the path splits left and right. Turn left and follow the path as it snakes its way up through the forest. Eventually you will reach a junction where you need to turn left and make your way downhill, this time with the Spinkwee River below you on your right.

6 A short distance down this section of the trail, you will see steps leading down into a viewing platform where you have spectacular views of the beautiful Cascade Waterfall.

7 Re-joining the trail, continue downhill and you will reach the Altavaddy Bridge, which will cross you over onto the right hand bank of the river. Follow the trail as you now make your way down the opposite river bank, passing two sets of stepping stones.

The Shimna River with the stepping stones in the distance.

The stepping stones and the meeting of the rivers.

8 The path makes its way round towards the lake, on your right hand side, and veers left and crosses back over the river using the Old Bridge.

Foley's Bridge.

Cascade Waterfall.

9 Upon reaching the opposite, immediately turn left and follow the path down to Foley's Bridge, which is one of the highlights of Tollymore Forest.

10 When finished, retrace your steps back to the Old Bridge, and then follow the trail uphill to your right which will return you to the main car park.

9 Hare's Gap – Commedagh

A tough and demanding walk, taking you along the Brandy Pad and then along the Mourne Wall

Not the best walk for those who are inexperienced or who don't have a relative degree of fitness. Enjoy the views from the Brandy Pad before reaching the col between Donard and Commedagh and then making your way along the famous Mourne Wall. Challenging yet very rewarding.

The walk begins at the car park (as in Walk 4) on the Trassey Road (311314), quite close to the Clonachullion Hill. There is adequate parking, but as noted before, at peak times and bank holidays, the car park will fill up quickly so you may have to park along the roadside as this is a very popular starting point for Mourne walkers.

Level: 🥾 🥾 🥾
Length: approx 10 – 11km
Time: approx 5 – 6 hours
Terrain: Moderate / Strenuous
Nearest Refreshments: Newcastle

Kilkeel River

The Mourne Wall

① Leaving the car park, turn left and walk a short distance up the Trassey Road until you come to a set of double gates and stile, which indicates the start of the Trassey Track. You will now begin a gradual ascent up a reasonably narrow stoned lane way before you reach a clearing where you will be greeted by a fine view of Slieve Meelmore, Slieve Bearnagh and Slievenaglogh (from right to left). Slieve Meelmore and Slieve Bearnagh are separated by the col at Pollaphuca while the col at the Hare's Gap separates the peaks of Bearnagh and Slievenaglogh. Again, you will come to a set of double gates and a stile. Please keep the gates closed and use the stile.

Continue up the narrow track as it begins a gradual ascent, with better views of the granite cliff face of Spellack, which is part of Slieve Meelmore, to your right. The track provides reasonably good footing, although there may be a few loose stones here and there.

② You will come to another stile and set of double gates, and then the path begins to wind its way uphill with the surface becoming a little more loose under foot. The Trassey Track continues to snake its way up towards the Hare's Gap, with the Trassey River running on your right hand side. You will come to a crossing

The view up towards Slieve Meelmore.

point in the river, which you cross and continue for approximately another 95 metres until you come to a fork in the path. To veer right would take you up towards the quarry nestled on the side of Slieve Bearnagh. However, you take the left fork, which leads you onto your final ascent up a reasonably steep boulder field to the Mourne Wall and the Hare's Gap, nestled between Slievenaglogh to your left and Slieve Bearnagh to your right. Care should be taken on this final ascent as the footing can be uneven and slippery. Don't forget to stop and catch your breath and look back on the stunning views overlooking Slievenaman and Lough Island Reavy Reservoir which will now be visible in the distance. On the final approach, fantastic views are also available of Slieve Bearnagh to your right, which some consider to be the most impressive of the peaks due to its summit tors, crags and smooth rock slabs.

Looking up to the col between Bearnagh and Meelmore.

3 Upon reaching the Mourne Wall, cross through the gate or use the stile and look for the path that leads off to your left. This is known as the Brandy Pad, which was used years ago to smuggle goods inland from the coast.

4 Stick to this path as it makes its way along the side of the mountains, with breath-taking views to your right looking down the valley towards Ben Crom Reservoir and the rugged tors of Slieve Binnian in the distance. This has got to be one of the most amazing panoramic views of the Mournes.

5 As you begin to approach the col between Slieve Commedagh to your left and Slieve Beg to your right, the path will begin to get a little steeper and will then drop down again as you pass round the side of Slieve Commedagh. Slieve Donard will now be visible straight ahead.

Slieve Bearnagh.

One of the best views in the Mournes, looking towards Ben Crom Reservoir in the distance.

Late evening light along the Brandy Pad.

Continue forward on the Brandy Pad, passing The Castles on your left. After a short distance you will see the col between Donard and Commedagh on your left hand side, with the Mourne Wall and a stile. Cut across leaving the Brandy Pad and make your way to the

Mourne Wall and cross the stile.

6 You now turn left and keeping the Mourne Wall to your left, make your way up to the summit of Slieve Commedagh reaching a height of 765 metres.

7 From the summit of Slieve Commedagh, follow the Mourne Wall which will take you along Slieve Corragh and Slievenaglogh. This section runs roughly parallel with the Brandy Pad and is an alternative return route back to the Hare's Gap. Remember to enjoy the excellent views!

8 When you reach the next stile, cross back over onto the opposite side of the Mourne Wall and descend slowly to the Hare's Gap.

You can now return down the way you came up until you reach the Trassey Road car park.

Moody clouds over Slieve Beg and the Devil's Coachroad.

10 **Slieve Loughshannagh**

Providing great views of Slieve Bearnagh and Slieve Binnian, this walk takes you along several peaks

Level: 🐾 🐾 🐾
Length: approx 11 km
Time: approx 5 hours
Terrain: Moderate / Difficult
Nearest Refreshments: Newcastle

E xperience the exhilaration of reaching several summits on this walk, as well as experiencing the beauty of Lough Shannagh and Slieve Bearnagh. This walk is quite demanding, especially on the last third as you follow the Mourne Wall prior to your descent.

The walk begins at the car park on the Trassey Road known as Happy Valley car park (293296). As with most Mourne car parks, you are advised to get there early.

The Mourne Wall.

59

① Leaving the car park, follow the path that leads to a gate and stile. Cross the stile and continue to follow the stony path uphill. After a short distance, you will notice another stile to your left, on the opposite bank of the stream. This stile actually marks the end point of your walk (to its left you will see a stone wall which runs back around Slieve Meelmore and towards the Trassey River). Continue on the path uphill for another 15 or 20 metres, and then descend towards the stream and find a suitable crossing point. You need to cross the stream and follow the wall upwards as it leads you up the valley between Slieve Meelmore (on your left) and Slieve Meelbeg (on your right).

The view looking back down the valley towards the Trassey Road.

The view up to the col between Slieve Meelbeg on the right and Slieve Meelmore on the left.

The Mourne Wall with Slieve Binnian and Doan and Ben Crom in the distance.

This path is very narrow at times, but always keep the stream on your right and keep the wall close on your left. Don't forget to turn around and enjoy the views back to the valley towards the Trassey Road and Slievenaman. As the wall winds its way upwards, the ascent gradually becomes much steeper.

2 The wall takes a sharp turn to the left as it heads up the side of Slieve Meelmore to meet the Mourne Wall, and it is this section which provides a bit of a physical challenge. But the views will make up for any tiredness or aches and pains in the legs.

When you reach the main Mourne Wall, looking to your right, you can see the wall run right across to the summit of Slieve Meelbeg at a height of 708 metres. You also have great views looking over towards the Silent Valley Reservoir and Slieve Binnian. But one of the best views has to be that of the rugged peak of Slieve Bearnagh straight ahead.

Looking towards Slieve Bearnagh.

(4) When you reach this other wall, turn right and follow the path which winds its way along the bottom of Slieve Meelbeg (to your right).

(5) After passing the Blue Lough on your left, the path veers off right and then sweeps round left along the side of Slieve Loughshannagh. Towering off to your left is the summit of Doan. Again the path will veer right and begin to ascend up towards the Mourne Wall at the col between Carn Mountain and Slieve Loughshannagh. You should meet a stile at this point in the wall.

(3) You now need to cross the wall and, instead of turning left and following the wall to the summit of Slieve Meelmore which you did in Walk 6, follow the wall straight ahead. DO NOT turn left.

Descend carefully as the footing can be quite difficult and loose in places. Stick to the wall until it reaches the Mourne Wall and the col between Slieve Meelmore and Slieve Bearnagh.

6 From here, turn right and follow the wall till you reach the summit of Slieve Loughshannagh at 619 metres. From here, continue following the wall and you will reach the summit of Slieve Meelbeg at 708 metres.

7 Keeping the Mourne Wall on your left, continue forward and as you drop down from the summit of Slieve Meelbeg, you will come to a stile, which you will cross, so that the Mourne Wall is now on your right.

There is no path at this point, but descend gradually until you reach the wall which you went up near the start. Follow this wall back down to the Happy Valley car park.

Your descent via this wall back to the Happy Valley car park.